Princess 1

'I don't think many people will want ... *things differently — I don't go by a rule book.'*

Diana Spencer was the beautiful English princess who changed the picture of the Royal Family. She did not become the Queen of Britain, but to the people of the country she did become a 'Queen of Hearts'.

She grew up almost next door to the Royal Family. But she didn't guess that one day she would be a princess too. Prince Charles was already a young man when she was only a little girl.

This story tells how they met and married. It tells how she brought new colour to the Royal Family, and also of the more serious side of her life. Diana wanted to change things in the world, and she helped many people through her work for charity.

Sadly, her fairy-tale marriage went wrong, and she learnt to live and work alone. But she was still so popular that reporters and photographers followed her everywhere. They were following her car when it crashed in Paris in August 1997. The accident killed Diana and her new boyfriend, Dodi.

Her life ended when she was 36, but people will remember her for ever.

Cherry Gilchrist was born in 1949, and lives in Bristol, England. She has written nineteen books, some for children. She also sells Russian paintings, and goes to Russia often. She likes to travel, and to visit old cities and interesting countries. When she has time, she also enjoys cooking and singing. Her husband writes about money, her son works with computers, and her daughter is a student at university.

For a complete list of the titles available in the Penguin Readers series please write to the following address for a catalogue: Penguin ELT Marketing Department, Penguin Books Ltd, 27 Wrights Lane, London W8 5TZ.

Princess Diana

CHERRY GILCHRIST

Level 3

Series Editors: Andy Hopkins and Jocelyn Potter

Addison Wesley Longman Limited
Edinburgh Gate, Harlow,
Essex CM20 2JE, England
and Associated Companies throughout the world.

ISBN 0 582 40204 2

First published by Penguin Books 1998
This edition first published 1998

Text copyright © Cherry Gilchrist 1998
Photographs copyright © Camera Press Limited
All rights reserved

Typeset by Digital Type, London
Set in 11/14pt Bembo
Reproduction by Anglia Graphics
Printed in Spain by Mateu Cromo, S.A. Pinto (Madrid)

Published by Addison Wesley Longman Limited in association with
Penguin Books Ltd., both companies being subsidiaries of Pearson Plc

Dictionary words:

- When you read this book, you will find that some words are darker black than the others on the page. Look them up in your dictionary, if you do not already know them, or try to guess the meaning of the words first, without a dictionary.

Diana, Princess of Wales 1961–1997.

CHAPTER ONE

The Girl with a Future

On 1 July 1961, a baby girl was born at her family home, in Sandringham, Norfolk. Her parents, Frances and Johnnie Spencer, couldn't decide what to call her at first. They had two daughters already, and this time they really wanted a boy. Finally, they called her 'Diana'. They didn't know that in the **future** the name Diana Spencer would be famous all over the world. They could not guess how **popular** she would be in her short but full **life**.

The Spencers are a very old English family. They became rich a long time ago as sheep farmers, and the family goes back to King Charles II and King James II of England. They have been friends and helpers of the **Royal** Family for hundreds of years.

The house they lived in then, Park House, was near the Queen's house at Sandringham, so Diana grew up almost 'next door' to the Royal Family. Diana often visited them at Sandringham House when she was a little girl. The Queen's most important homes are at Buckingham Palace★ in London, and Windsor Castle† just to the west of London. But she also spends time at Balmoral Castle in Scotland, and at Sandringham House, which is in the east of England.

Later, people called Diana 'a **fairy-tale** princess'. But her story was often a sad one too. Her parents had the son that they wanted so much in 1964 – they called him Charles. But their **marriage** was unhappy, and soon terrible fights began. When Diana was only six, her mother, Frances, ran away with another man, Peter Shand Kydd.

★ A palace is a large house where an important family, like the Royal Family, lives.
† A castle is a large building, usually very old, which could once keep an enemy out.

For a long time, the children could only visit their mother at weekends. Frances very much wanted her children to live with her. But their father was against the idea, and so they stayed at Park House with him. Other women came to the house to look after the children, but they didn't usually stay long. The children made trouble for them – they threw their clothes out of the window, or locked them in the toilet! The two smallest children, Charles and Diana, were really unhappy. Each night in bed, Charles cried for his mother, and Diana lay there **alone**, listening to him. She was too frightened of the dark house to get out of bed and go to him.

But Diana and Charles were a loving brother and sister. As time went on, they often travelled by train together to visit their mother. Diana was always friendly with her two older sisters, Sarah and Jane, but they had different lives.

Johnnie Spencer tried to do his best for the four children, and at Christmas they could choose all the presents that they wanted. There were too many presents, and not enough **hugs** and kisses, they remembered later. Diana loved her father, and wanted to look after him. She liked to help in the house too, and to look after her animals. She had a cat, Marmalade, and a dog called Jill. Like a lot of English girls, Diana learned to ride a horse, but after she broke her arm in an accident she was frightened, and didn't want to ride again.

Like the children in many rich or old families in England, the Spencer children went away to school. Diana went to Riddlesworth Hall School in 1970 when she was only seven. She lived there during the term, and came home in the holidays. In 1974 she went on to her mother's old school, West Heath School in Kent, which was on the other side of London from Norfolk. Her sisters Sarah and Jane were also students there.

By then, her mother wasn't living in London, but in Scotland. She and her husband Peter had a large farm on an island. It was a

Diana and Charles were a loving brother and sister.

wild and beautiful place, and Diana had some lovely holidays there.

In Diana's young life, everything was always changing, and she often felt alone. She was very sad when her grandmother – her father's mother – died in 1972. Her grandmother was a very kind woman. She looked after Diana a lot when her parents **separated**. Things changed even more in 1975 when her grandfather died too, and the Spencer family moved into the old family home at Althorp, in Northamptonshire. Diana's father was now

Earl★ Spencer, Diana became Lady★ Diana Spencer, and her brother Charles a Viscount.★ Later, he too became an Earl.

Until then, Park House in Sandringham was the only home that Diana knew. She didn't like going to Sandringham House to visit the royal family much – she felt strange in the royal house. But she loved Park House, with its friendly rooms and its big garden. She could go swimming in the pool there, play tennis, or hide in the tree-house. The children didn't really want to live at Althorp. They didn't enjoy their visits there when their grandfather was alive. The house was large, dark and frightening, with lots of old family pictures on the walls. But as they grew up, they liked it more. They enjoyed having their friends to stay – it was a good house for parties!

At school, Diana made plenty of friends. She was a good student, not especially clever, but she enjoyed her lessons. She liked English and painting, but she was best at dancing and swimming. It was soon clear that she would never go to university, but she was helpful and kind. She even won a cup for helpfulness! As part of the school's **charity** programme, Diana began to visit old or ill people in the town near the school. Usually, she talked to them, or helped with their shopping. This is perhaps where her love of charity work began.

But she was not always quite so good. Once she got into real trouble when she left the school at night! She planned to meet a friend outside the school to get some sweets from her. One of the teachers found her empty bed and called the police! The head teacher was very angry, but her parents were secretly amused.

When Diana left West Heath School, she was sixteen. At first she didn't know what to do. Life at home was changing again because her father had a new wife. Her name was Raine, and she was the daughter of Barbara Cartland, a famous writer of love

★ Earl, Lady and Viscount are some of the names which important English families use, instead of Mr, Mrs or Miss.

4

stories. Diana and her brother and sisters were not very pleased about the marriage. They didn't want Raine as their second mother, and were always fighting with her.

But Johnnie loved his new wife, and they were very happy together. And, in the end, Diana was pleased that Raine was there to look after her father. In 1978, a year after the marriage, Johnnie became very ill. The doctors thought that he would die. Raine nursed him back to health, but it was a long time before he was better again.

A little earlier, in 1977, Diana went off to a very expensive 'finishing' school in Switzerland because she didn't want to stay at home. Girls from rich families went there to learn to cook, to speak French, and to look after a home. Diana only stayed there for six weeks, then decided that she wanted to go back to England to work. In the past, girls from important families like the Spencers never worked for money. But times were different now, and Diana wanted to be like other girls of her age.

'I can easily find a job,' she told her father.

He bought her a very nice flat in Coleherne Court, Kensington, in the centre of London. She asked a few friends to come and live with her – one of them, Carolyn Pride, was an old schoolfriend of hers.

This was the beginning of a really happy time for Diana. She was young and pretty. She had good friends – both boyfriends and girlfriends – and a nice flat and a car. She was free to try and find her way in the world.

What could she do for a job? She loved children, and so she began to look after babies and small children for her sisters' friends. Sometimes she cleaned their houses too, or cooked meals for them. She studied cooking again in London – she was good at Russian soup; but she and the girls in the flat ate chocolate most of the time!

Then she found a job at the Young England School for little

children. Here she was very happy, and her bosses were very pleased with her work. She was calm and kind with the children, and always gave them plenty of love and hugs.

Soon there would be love in her life too – she would find her prince and fall in love. She would become the new Princess of Wales. She didn't know this, of course, but she *did* feel that she was getting ready for something special. Diana went to parties, and she had a lot of friends, but she was never serious about a man at that time.

'I had to keep myself tidy,' she said later, 'for what was coming.'

CHAPTER TWO

A Fairy-Tale Wedding

Prince Charles was taking a long time to choose a wife. He was already 32. He always had plenty of girlfriends – Diana's sister, Sarah, was once his girlfriend. But he couldn't decide who to marry. Charles was the future King of Britain, so he had to choose well. Not every beautiful woman makes a good queen. Life in the Royal Family can be very hard – the 'Royals' spend a lot of time in **public**. She must also be a girl from a good family, and Charles must be her first lover.

In February 1981, the news finally came out that Prince Charles was getting married – to Lady Diana Spencer. The photos in the newspapers showed a pretty, quiet girl with a sweet smile, and the reporters soon began to call her 'Shy Di'. Diana was the first English girl to marry a Prince of Wales for five hundred years. And in **private**, Prince Charles said that the Spencers were 'more royal than the Royals'! It seemed that Diana and Charles were perfect together. People in Britain began to look forward to a fairy-tale wedding.

The photos in the newspapers showed a pretty, quiet girl with a sweet smile, and the reporters soon began to call her 'Shy Di'.

Diana grew up with the Royal Family, but for a long time she didn't really know Charles. There are a lot of families in the royal circle, and also Charles was twelve years older than her. He was already a young man when she was still a child. But when Diana was sixteen, they met at a country house party. She was only a schoolgirl, and Charles was more interested in his dog and his sport than in her. But from that time, Diana put a photo of Charles by her bed.

They met at a few more parties, but it was only in July 1980 that Charles began to look at Diana with new eyes. They were both staying with friends in the country. In the evening, Diana sat next to Charles outside in the garden. She was telling him that she saw him at a **funeral** a year earlier.

'You looked so sad,' she said. 'I thought, "It's wrong that you're alone – you need someone to look after you."'

Charles's heart opened to her, and from then on he was seriously interested in her. He asked her out for an evening of music, with supper later at Buckingham Palace. But he didn't give Diana much time – she only had twenty minutes to wash her hair and get ready!

'Maybe you'll be the next Queen of England!' a friend told her. Diana only laughed.

Then Charles asked her to go to Balmoral for the Braemar Games, the Scottish sports which happen every September. Diana's sister Jane was now married to Robert Fellowes, the Queen's personal secretary. They had a small house in the royal park at Balmoral, and Diana stayed there with her sister and husband. Prince Charles phoned her every day, and they went for walks together.

Until then, no one guessed that the Prince had a new girlfriend. But, one day, Charles and Diana were fishing down by the River Dee. Suddenly they noticed someone on the other side of the river. It was a reporter from a newspaper looking for royal news. Diana quickly ran to hide behind some trees, and used a mirror from her handbag to watch him. Two other photographers hurried to the same place by the river. They were all very excited, trying to see this new woman in Charles's life. Diana escaped from them that day. But soon the reporters knew her name, and it was in all the newspapers.

Now her life began to change. The public wanted to know all about her, and paparazzi★ followed her everywhere. They followed her in her little red Mini-Metro car. They phoned her in the middle of the night and waited for her outside the Young England School. Even when she agreed to a photograph, they still made trouble. The light was shining behind her skirt and showed all of

★ Paparazzi – an Italian word for the reporters and photographers who follow famous people and try to sell their stories and pictures for a lot of money to the newspapers.

her long, beautiful legs! It was a very difficult time for a shy young girl, and the Royal Family didn't help her. Even Charles was not amused by the photograph. Diana began to understand that even famous and popular people can be very much alone.

When Prince Charles finally asked her to marry him, in February 1981, she agreed. She arrived back at her flat very happy that night. Her friends were waiting for her. They knew that it was something special!

Diana said, 'I've got news for you – but I must go to the toilet first!'

So they all knocked on the toilet door until she told them!

'I'm going to marry Prince Charles!' she called out, half-laughing and half-crying.

He gave her a beautiful blue ring, and they were ready now for the photographs, the television **recordings** and the public **appearances**. Several times, they had to answer the question, 'Are you in love?'

'Of course!' answered Diana.

But Charles was not so sure. His answer always seemed to be, 'Yes – but what does that mean?'

To the public, it *was* real love. It was exciting news for Britain. Here was a fairy-tale prince and princess, bringing new colour and life into the Royal Family.

Diana now moved into Clarence House, the Queen Mother's home, and was safer there from the reporters. Everyone was getting ready for the wedding – over ten-thousand presents arrived for Charles and Diana! She chose a young husband and wife, David and Elizabeth Emanuel, to make her wedding dress.

'She made coffee for us,' they remembered. 'Here was the future Princess of Wales, and we were students not so long ago. It was quite a surprise.'

But not everything was perfect. At the centre of the fairy-tale, there was a black shadow. When Charles asked Diana to marry

Charles gave her a beautiful blue ring, and they were ready now for the photographs.

him, something strange happened. She suddenly felt, deep inside, that she would never be Queen. She also knew that she would have a difficult job as Charles's wife.

This did not stop her. But, just before the wedding, she became seriously worried. She suddenly understood that Charles's old girlfriend, Camilla Parker-Bowles, was still very important to him. Diana found a present from Charles to Camilla, and he often telephoned her. Did Charles really love her, or was he still in love with Camilla?

And Diana was no longer free. The happy days in her flat with her friends, and at work with the little children, were all gone. The 'royal machine' frightened her. There were so many royal rules, and Buckingham Palace was a 'dead' place to her. No one welcomed her when she arrived at Clarence House, and no one told her how to do things.

She still tried to enjoy herself. She escaped to Australia for a quiet holiday with her mother where none of the paparazzi could find them. Back at Clarence House, she wanted to go on with her dancing, and so she asked her old teacher to come and work with her. But she knew that soon nothing would be the same. During one of her last lessons she said, 'In twelve days' time, I shall no longer be me.'

She got thinner, and she even wanted to stop the wedding. Her sisters told her to go on.

'Bad luck – you've got to do it! Your face is on the tea-towels now!' they said.

So on 29 July 1981, Prince Charles married Lady Diana Spencer in St Paul's Cathedral, London. It was a great day for England. More than a million people were out on the streets in the morning to wave as she went by. In Britain, everything stopped as people switched on the television. In many houses there were little parties as families, friends and neighbours all sat down together to enjoy themselves.

Diana arrived at St Paul's with her father. The church was full of important people from all over the world. Not only was the British Royal Family there, but there were other kings and queens from Europe. There was beautiful music, and the church was full of flowers. Diana looked wonderful in her long wedding dress, which was almost white, with the skirt very long at the back. With flowers in her hands, and her heart full of hope, she agreed to marry Charles.

'I will,' she said.

Charles put the wedding ring on her finger. It was made of Welsh gold. This gold was a present to the Royal Family about fifty years earlier, and Diana's ring was made of the very last piece.

Charles and Diana were now husband and wife. They promised to stay together all their lives.

The crowds who were shouting 'Lady Di! Lady Di!' now changed the words to 'Princess Di! Princess Di!'

They went back to Buckingham Palace, where Charles kissed his new wife in public. Then they left for their wedding holiday, first at a house called Broadlands, then on the royal ship, *Britannia*.

Diana was suddenly the world's favourite woman. Her face really was on the tea-towels – and on cups, glasses, spoons, and all kinds of things that people bought at the time of the Royal Wedding. They wanted something to record and remember that special day, the most important royal day since Elizabeth became Queen in June 1953.

In some ways, Queen Elizabeth was still part of a picture which was painted by the famous Queen Victoria over a hundred years before. In this picture, the Royal Family is a good Christian family. They show a polite face in public, and keep all their problems secret. Royal children must learn that their country comes first, and their personal life second. Sadly, this can also give us a Royal Family which seems cold and far away.

Queen Elizabeth did try to make the Royal Family more

Charles and Diana were now husband and wife. They promised to stay together all their lives.

modern. Once, most royal children studied at home, but her son Prince Charles went away to school and university. In the 1960s television cameras recorded her home and her family life for the first time, so that people began to know the Royal Family a little bit better. But, in the end, it was not enough for modern times.

So could the fairy-tale marriage possibly have a happy ending? Did Charles really love Diana when he married her? He probably tried to do his best at the time, but it was difficult for him, too. In the past, kings and princes married to make the Royal Family stronger and to have children. Now Charles had to find the right wife for the Royal Family, *and* marry for love. Could Diana be the perfect royal wife, when she was also a modern girl? In 1981, we didn't ask ourselves these questions. We all wanted to enjoy the fairy tale while we could.

CHAPTER THREE

The Young Princess

In her new marriage, Diana was like a young bird who was learning to fly. At school, she was too shy to speak in public. Now she was making public appearances all the time as one of the Royal Family. One of her first public visits was in May just before she got married. This was to Tetbury, a town near Prince Charles's new country home at Highgrove in Gloucestershire. Crowds of people came out to see Diana. Dressed in a red suit, she walked through the streets and smiled shyly as they gave her bunches of flowers.

It took some time before she wasn't frightened of these public appearances. On one of the first that she made with Prince Charles, he told her to walk over to the waiting crowds.

'Talk to them,' he told her.

'I can't! I just can't!' she said.

But she had to, and after that, she found it became easier and easier. She was very natural, and everyone liked that. People began to feel that they could talk to her about their problems. She was quickly becoming one of the most popular women in the world.

Soon she was more popular than Charles. He wasn't very pleased by this.

'I'm sorry I'm not my wife,' he said once or twice to the crowds when he made visits alone.

Everyone loved Diana because she was young and beautiful. During her first few years as a princess, she learnt how to dress well, and people became interested in her clothes. After every appearance, the reporters described what she was wearing. There were photos in the newspapers recording all her different dresses. Before she got married, she still looked very young. Her face was round, and her clothes were nothing special. And when she first became Princess of Wales, she still didn't always dress well. Sometimes she wore dresses and hats that were too old for her, like those for a 45-year-old woman.

Then she became the well-dressed Diana that we remember today. She chose a lot of wonderful clothes – dinner dresses, dance dresses, trousers, and suits. She learnt to dress for all kinds of different appearances – for special visits, for sports, or for travel. For public appearances, she had to wear clothes that were comfortable, as well as beautiful. She also had to remember how her enemy, the wind, could blow those clothes about!

Diana began to buy from famous British clothes-makers, which helped the clothes business in Britain. Some of her favourites were Bruce Oldfield, Zandra Rhodes, and Catherine Walker. Sometimes she chose bravely – a low-cut, short black dress, for example. But she could also look like the perfect 'English rose' in a pink, well-cut suit, or a long white dance dress. With her long legs, fair hair and wonderful smile, she could look good in almost anything.

Diana began to buy from famous British clothes-makers. Sometimes she chose bravely – a low-cut, short black dress, for example.

Then Diana became a mother too. Before the baby was born, she felt sick a lot of the time. But she was healthy, and on 21 June 1982, she went into St Mary's Hospital, London to have her baby. Charles stayed with her there, and the Queen's private doctor looked after her. At 9.03 p.m., the new prince was born. Crowds were waiting outside.

'Nice one, Charlie!' they shouted when they heard the news.

'He's got fair hair,' the proud father told them.

At first the new parents couldn't agree on names. Charles wanted to call the baby Arthur, but Diana preferred William. On 3 August, in the Music Room at Buckingham Palace, they gave their son the names William Arthur Philip Louis.

Diana's first big public visit was to Australia, New Zealand and Canada early in 1983. Usually, royal babies and small children stayed at home when their parents went to other countries. When Prince Charles was only a little boy, for example, his mother Queen Elizabeth went away for several months. And when they finally met again, she only shook his hand. Diana was a different kind of mother. She wanted to keep her children with her, and to give them plenty of love. She wasn't afraid to hug and kiss them in public.

So Charles and Diana took baby William with them. Great crowds came out to see the Prince and Princess of Wales, and Diana quickly became popular in those countries too. She was always ready to do what people liked best – on her first visit to Wales, she spoke in Welsh. Then, in New Zealand, she met a Maori woman, and touched noses to say 'Hello', in the local way.

Soon another baby was coming, and on 15 September 1984 Prince Harry was born. When the family was in London, they lived in a large flat at Kensington Palace. It had four sitting-rooms, a dining-room, and four bedrooms. Diana chose all the colours and the furniture, and tried to make it a real family home.

Here she looked after her boys. She often played with them,

Diana often played with William and Harry, and helped them with their early lessons.

and helped them with their early lessons. But it was important that they met other children too. Charles wanted William and Harry to study at home with a private teacher, but Diana didn't agree. So in September 1985, William went to his first school. In 1987, he went on to Wetherby School. On his first day, she took him there just like any other mother, and together they met his new teacher.

Diana was now a busy princess, wife and mother. But she was beginning to work with charities now too, which quickly became one of the most important things in her life. In 1982, the newspapers reported that Diana was now working with five charities. By the time that she was 24, she was working with eighteen. She began to visit people in hospital. She wasn't afraid to meet people who were dying. And she began to meet people with terrible illnesses like AIDS.★ A lot of people were frightened that you could catch AIDS by touching someone; Diana held the hand of a man with AIDS to show that this wasn't true. The photographs of this helped people with AIDS a lot.

She worked hard, but she still wanted to have a good time too. She practised a special dance secretly with the famous dancer, Wayne Sleep. Then, one night at the theatre, she suddenly went up to the front to dance with Wayne. She wanted to surprise Prince Charles! The newspapers were full of it the next day. Only Prince Charles was not so pleased. In private, he told her that it was not the right thing for a princess to do.

Diana now had a new friend in the Royal Family. This was Sarah Ferguson, or 'Fergie', who married Prince Andrew, Charles's younger brother, in 1986. She was a girl with a warm heart, but she wasn't always sensible. One night, just before they got married, Prince Andrew was having a 'men only' party. 'Fergie' and Diana dressed up as policewomen to try and get in! Again, the

★ AIDS – the dangerous illness which you can catch from someone's blood, or from making love with them.

Royal Family were not pleased with Diana. She was becoming too wild . . .

Few people knew that at this time Diana was not happy. She seemed to have the perfect life. But inside she was in trouble. She was helping other people, but she needed help herself. She was popular, a great favourite of the people, and reporters photographed her everywhere. But in private, she was alone with her troubles.

CHAPTER FOUR

The Woman Inside

In November 1982, the Palace told the world that Diana was 'in the best of health'. She did not have an eating illness, as some of the newspapers were saying.

Diana began to look too thin even before she got married. People thought that she was just tired, or growing up. But in fact, Diana *was* getting ill. She ate too much, then made herself sick. She ate large meals out of the refrigerator late at night. She ate cakes and chocolate, and was sometimes sick several times a day. At first she looked thin because she kept no food down inside her. But in the end, she learnt to hide her illness so that she looked fine.

In January 1982, Diana fell down some stairs when her first baby was on the way. It wasn't in the newspapers until a few weeks later. It was an accident, the Palace said. It was only a few stairs. The doctor visited her and she was fine now. There was nothing to worry about.

But Diana tried to kill herself that day. Life was too much for her. She felt sick all the time before William was born, and her new 'job' in the Royal Family was very difficult. Most of all, she felt that her husband wasn't really interested in her. On that day, he wanted to go out horse-riding, and he wouldn't stay to talk to her.

After William was born, she felt very unhappy. This happens to many women, of course, for a short time after they have babies. But Diana got worse, not better. She sometimes cut herself with a knife, and tried several more times to kill herself. She was probably crying out for help. Outside, she was still the perfect Princess of Wales, but inside, she was hurting.

Before Prince Harry was born, the hospital told Diana that the baby was a boy. She didn't tell Charles. He really wanted a girl. When he first saw their new son, he told her this. Suddenly Diana felt that this was the end of their marriage.

'Something inside me died,' she told her friends later.

She married for love, but perhaps Charles didn't. Did his family push him into the marriage? His real love, Camilla Parker-Bowles, was already married, and he had to marry someone. Perhaps he chose Diana only because she would be the right sort of royal wife and mother.

Charles was still seeing Camilla when he was married to Diana. On their wedding holiday, Diana saw that Charles still kept photos of Camilla in his pocket. And during the marriage, Charles still gave Camilla presents, and often telephoned her privately.

The mother of Camilla's grandmother also had a royal lover, King Edward VII. Camilla, it seemed, was repeating the family story. But Charles and Camilla were friends, as well as lovers. They were the same age, and they were interested in the same things, like horses and the country. Many women did not find Charles an easy man, but Camilla seemed to understand him well. Earlier, a lot of his girlfriends got tired of him. He could be warm one day, and cold the next. He spent time with them, then disappeared for a long time. Even Camilla stopped waiting for him when she was young. She married another man, Andrew Parker-Bowles.

Charles and Diana were different ages, and they liked different

Camilla Parker-Bowles. Charles and Camilla were friends,
as well as lovers. They were the same age, and they were
interested in the same things.

things. He wanted to read books on their wedding holiday; Diana wanted to enjoy the sun and the sea. He wanted to talk about serious ideas, when she wanted to give everything to their new love. It was soon clear to them both that they thought and felt very differently.

In public, they were still husband and wife, but in private they were sleeping in separate bedrooms. People were beginning to see that all was not well. In Canada in 1986, Diana fell down in public because she was so ill and unhappy. The same year, Prince Charles came home early from their holiday in Majorca. Then, in 1987, he went up to Balmoral alone for a month. He told the reporters that he had a lot of work to do there.

Diana was working hard for the Royal Family and the country, but she was still very unsure of herself. She was always waiting for Charles and the Royal Family to say 'Well done!' They never did. But in 1988, life began to change for her. She found that she could be strong.

A terrible accident happened when she and Charles were on holiday in Switzerland with a group of friends. Snow came down from the mountains and killed Hugh Lindsay, one of their best friends. Diana was in bed with a cold at the time. One of Charles's secretaries arrived back at the house with the terrible news.

Diana decided what she needed to do. She put all Lindsay's clothes into his suitcase. She and Charles flew back to England with the body. Then Diana looked after Hugh Lindsay's wife, Sarah. The Lindsays only got married a few months before the holiday, and Sarah was having a baby.

And then Diana decided that it was time to help herself, too. Carolyn, her old schoolfriend, said, 'I'll give you an hour. If you don't go to a doctor, I'll tell the world about your illness!'

Diana went to see a special doctor for help with her eating illness.

'How many times have you tried to kill yourself?' he asked her at once.

'Four or five times,' she said. She was very surprised that he seemed to know all about her so quickly.

In six months' time, he told her, she could be a new person. He visited her every week, and she began to read books about the illness and to understand herself better. In six months, she *was* a new person, and she was almost better.

It was the beginning of a new way of life for her. She *had* to help herself; Charles wouldn't help her. He didn't love her as she wanted. And he never would.

She also learnt to give her love to the poor and ill people that she met through her charity work. She had a special touch. When she visited people in hospital, a hug or a kiss from Diana seemed to help them greatly. Sometimes she continued to visit people for a long time until they were better. She often wrote them kind letters later. A lot of her charity work was with children, and she was always happy and natural with them.

At home, it was the beginning of the war between Diana and the Royal Family. It was difficult for people who worked for Charles and Diana. They had to decide which side they were on. You had to be a 'Charles person' or a 'Diana person'. If you tried to be both, you quickly got into trouble. Diana began to think of 'Charles's people' as 'the enemy.'

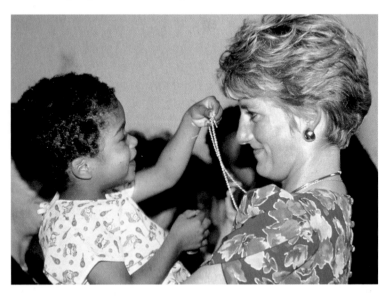

A lot of Diana's charity work was with children, and she was always happy and natural with them.

They now lived two separate lives in the family too. There was Diana's life, and Charles's life. This was true even for the boys. When Diana took them out, they went to modern places that children like – water game parks or the cinema. They usually wore ordinary clothes like jeans and T-shirts. With Charles, they wore more grown-up clothes, and did country things that he enjoyed, like fishing.

The public began to think worse of Charles when Prince William had a serious accident at school in 1991. Diana stayed at the hospital with him all night but Charles went off to the theatre.

'How could he do that?' people asked. 'What sort of a father is he?'

Charles loved his sons too, but perhaps he didn't understand how to show it. He did try to do better after that, but many people were beginning to prefer Diana.

But not everyone. 'She's ill,' some people were saying. 'She needs to be in hospital.' Or: 'She's trying to hurt the Royal Family. They must stop her!'

Diana was beginning to make a new life for herself. It was difficult, and she was often unhappy, but it was the only way out.

CHAPTER FIVE

The New Diana

The Queen called 1992 a 'terrible year'. It began badly for Diana, too. On 29 March, her much-loved father died. She was on holiday in Austria, and she flew home at once for the funeral. Prince Charles flew back with her to England, but she went to the funeral alone. The newspapers, of course, were quick to notice this.

It was a month for royal stories. The Palace told the world

that the marriage of Prince Andrew and Sarah Ferguson was over.

Then a new book came out about Princess Diana: *Diana – Her True Story* by Andrew Morton. The book talked about Diana's eating illness, and about how unhappy she was with Prince Charles and the Royal Family. It also talked about Prince Charles and Camilla Parker-Bowles. At first, everyone was very surprised. Could it all be true? In the end, people realised that most of it *was* Diana's real story.

But there was another surprise coming for her – and an unpleasant one. Diana was beginning, secretly, to look for a new love in her life. She had to be very careful, because she and Charles were still married. The world would not think well of a royal mother with other lovers. Then suddenly, recordings of secret phone calls between Diana and James Gilbey came out. Gilbey was an old friend of Diana's, but here they were talking as lovers. Someone recorded the conversations, the newspapers said, two years earlier.

In them, Gilbey uses a special name for Diana – 'Squidgy'. He asks Diana to kiss him down the phone, and says, 'Oh Squidgy, I love you, love you, love you!'

Another lover was James Hewitt, the man who taught Diana to ride again – she was still afraid of horses after her accident as a child. Will Carling, the sportsman, and his wife ended their marriage because of Diana. Then there was Oliver Hoare, who sold paintings. Someone began to make silent phone calls to his home; perhaps it was Diana, unhappy because Oliver didn't want to talk to her. We will probably never know everything about her life at this time, but it's clear that she was seeing other men.

Then in 1993 recordings of phone conversations between Charles and Camilla appeared, and everyone now knew for sure that they *were* lovers. Charles was very unhappy about this, and at first promised to live alone without women. A year later he talked about it all on television. But he didn't stop seeing Camilla.

In the photos of 1992, Diana is often alone. In one, she is sitting in front of the Taj Mahal in India. She is smiling, but she looks very small and alone in front of the big white building. In November 1992, Charles and Diana did make a visit together to Korea, but they were clearly unhappy. Finally, in December they

In one photo Diana is sitting in front of the Taj Mahal. She is smiling, but she looks very small and alone in front of the big white building.

told the public that they were separating. Prince Charles would stay at Highgrove, and Diana would live alone at Kensington Palace. The children would spend time with both of their parents.

The Queen's family was in trouble all around her. Just to finish the terrible story of 1992, there was a serious fire at Windsor Castle, the Queen's favourite home. Everyone there, the Queen too, worked hard to put it out. But the Castle and the Royal Family would never be the same again.

♦

Diana's private rooms at Kensington Palace were full of photos of William and Harry.

'They mean everything to me,' she said. But now she couldn't be with them so much. A lot of the time, they were at school or with their father. She even had to eat her Christmas dinner alone while William and Harry spent Christmas day with their father and grandmother.

But she was doing her best to help her sons for their future as royal princes, and William perhaps as the future King of England. She decided that they needed to understand some of the country's problems. She took them to visit sick people in hospitals. But she also took them out secretly to see some of the dark and unpleasant places where homeless people spend the night. In 1995, William went to Eton, one of the top schools in the country, but he didn't forget the other side of life that Diana showed him. He later gave Diana the idea of selling a lot of her dresses for charity.

Diana's new life had good times in it, too. She had plenty of friends. Many of them were famous, and some of them were filmstars or popstars. She was friendly with the popstars Elton John and George Michael, and with Terence Stamp and Richard Attenborough, the filmstars. She knew Luciano Pavarotti, the Italian singer, and others from the music and film world, like Michael Jackson, Paul and Linda McCartney, and Liza Minelli. She often had lunch with friends. An Italian restaurant, San Lorenzo in Kensington was her favourite for a long time. She still loved dancing and pop music, and she went swimming or running every day to keep in good shape. Diana was very serious about her health now.

But she couldn't escape from the paparazzi. Everywhere she went, they tried to take photographs of her. Sometimes they took photos secretly – you could get a lot of money for a new photo of Diana.

Suddenly, it was all too much for her. In December 1993, she told the world that she wanted to live quietly. She would stop most of her work for charities. She needed time for her children, and for her private life.

It was not for long. She soon came back because she wanted to get on with her work, and be 'a mother to the world', as one newspaper wrote. And the story of Diana and Charles was not over yet; in November 1995 she recorded her famous appearance on television.

She talked openly to reporter Martin Bashir about her life in the Royal Family, and she was clearly hurt and angry about the past.

'There were three in this marriage,' she said about Charles and Camilla. And three, as she told us, is a crowd.

But she also talked about her future. 'I don't think many people will want me to be Queen ... because I do things differently, because I don't go by a rule book.' She worked, she said, 'from the heart, not the head'. But she wanted 'to be Queen of people's hearts'. These were words which the world never forgot.

A lot of people that she helped will never forget her either. One of her favourite charities was Centrepoint, which looks after homeless people. Vincent Seabrook, a man of 27 now working as a private guard, remembers her well. He was living homeless on the streets when Diana came past and stopped to talk to him.

On television Diana talked openly about her life in the Royal Family, and she was clearly hurt and angry about the past.

'She got me something to eat and drink, listened to me, and gave me the number for Centrepoint,' he said.

She wasn't frightened of illness, or of people who had serious problems with their bodies. She was ready with a hug or a kiss for everyone.

A man who couldn't see wanted to know what Diana was like. 'Is it all right if I touch your face?' he asked.

'Of course you can,' she said.

He moved his hands over her eyes, nose and mouth until he could see a picture of her in his head.

'You're very pretty!' he said.

When someone was in trouble, she tried to help them. Once in hospital, she heard a woman crying. The woman's son, Dean, was badly hurt in a car accident. Diana sat with the young man that night, and visited him again later. She even went to his house when he was better, and met his children.

'What shall we call you?' they all asked.

'Just Diana,' she said.

She often visited children's hospitals like Great Ormond Street Hospital for Sick Children. Victoria Hemphill, a young girl with a serious heart problem, felt that the Princess was her special friend, and kept photos of Diana by her bed. Diana often talked to her about William and Harry, and the boys wrote to her. 'Dearest Victoria, I wanted to send you lots of love while you were in hospital,' began a letter from Prince Harry.

Diana had time for her friends who were in trouble, too. She helped a friend called Rosa when her baby died, and gave time to another friend, Cosima, when her marriage ended. She knew what it was like to feel hurt inside.

She still travelled to other countries. In 1994 she visited Zimbabwe, in Africa. Photos show that she helped to give out lunch to children in a special school. She visited hospitals in Pakistan. In India, she became friends with Mother Teresa, who was famous for her work with poor people who were dying on the streets.

Diana once said, 'I'm not frightened of dying, if I can die happy.'

CHAPTER SIX

Her Last Days

After Diana's marriage finally ended in August 1996, she was a rich woman with over £17 million. But she wanted to go on working. She specially wanted to stop the use of landmines.* She visited Angola and Bosnia, where there are still terrible problems with landmines after the wars there. She met people who lost legs or arms from these landmines – not only men, but little children too. When she spoke out against the landmines, not everyone agreed with her. But Diana was still ready to speak from the heart.

She had a good summer in 1997. She visited her brother, Charles, in South Africa. She spent her birthday there, and enjoyed a holiday with Charles and his family without any of the usual trouble from the paparazzi.

There was only one sad time in the middle of July, when she went to Italy for the funeral of her friend Gianni Versace, the famous clothes-maker.

Something very special was happening in Diana's life that summer too. She had a new boyfriend. This was Dodi Al Fayed, a film-maker, who was 42. The Al Fayeds are a Moslem family from Egypt, but they live in England. They are very rich; the famous London shop, Harrods, and the Ritz Hotel in Paris belong to Mohammed Al Fayed, Dodi's father.

The Al Fayed family and the Spencer family were already friends. Diana first met Dodi about ten years earlier, but they didn't become good friends until she went on holiday to France with the Al Fayed family in July 1997. Harry and William went too, and they all had a wonderful time. It was the best holiday for years, Diana said later. And soon Diana and Dodi became more than friends; they fell in love.

They went away on holiday again at the end of that month, but they were alone together this time. They visited Corsica and Sardinia in the Al Fayeds' private boat. The paparazzi soon knew

* Landmines are put in the ground during the war to hurt the enemy, but they can hurt ordinary people too for a long time after the war because they don't always know where the landmines are.

that they were lovers. And then, of course, they all wanted to get pictures and stories of Diana and Dodi. The man who took the first photos of their kisses sold the pictures for a million dollars.

On 21 August, Diana flew back to France again to start a third holiday with Dodi. By now, they were deeply in love. He gave her presents, and it's possible that they planned to get married. Dodi was married before, and had a lot of girlfriends after that. But he was very serious about Diana.

This third holiday ended suddenly because of the paparazzi. When their boat arrived at Sardinia, the photographers ran after Dodi and Diana everywhere. They even found them at a hotel where they were staying secretly. That was enough — the lovers decided to leave at once for Paris.

They arrived on Saturday, 30 August. Dodi had a small home in Paris, which they tried to use secretly. During the afternoon, Dodi went out to get a very expensive ring which he was buying as a present for Diana. It was a ring that she would never wear.

The paparazzi knew Diana and Dodi were now in Paris and were following them again. They planned to eat dinner at a restaurant in the city centre, but decided that it wasn't safe there. They went on to the Ritz, the hotel which belongs to Dodi's father. When they arrived at the Ritz, there were already about 40 paparazzi waiting for them.

At last, just after midnight, they left the hotel by the back door to go back to Dodi's house. They were trying to escape, and sent off another car from the front. But some of the paparazzi saw Diana and Dodi as they drove off in their special Mercedes car with their driver and bodyguard.

'You won't catch me!' said the driver, Henri Paul, as he drove faster and faster; so did the paparazzi, some in cars, and several on very fast bikes. There were cameras and lights everywhere, as they tried to photograph Diana's car.

When the road came to the River Seine, it went underground.

The car was now travelling very fast – perhaps at over 160 km an hour. It hit a wall. The crash killed Dodi and the driver at once. The bodyguard, Trevor Rees-Jones, was still alive. So was Diana – but she was very badly hurt.

It took more than an hour before they could get her out of the crashed car. They took her to hospital, where doctors tried to save her life. But it was no good. She died at about four o'clock in the morning.

Soon telephones were ringing in Britain as people heard the news and phoned to tell their friends and families. Some heard it on the television or radio at the end of a long night's work, and it seemed that it couldn't possibly be true.

At Balmoral, Prince Charles woke his sons William and Harry to tell them the terrible news. That afternoon, Charles left Scotland by plane with Diana's two sisters Sarah and Jane. They flew to Paris together to bring her body home.

During the week, newspapers, television and radio were full of Diana's sad story. People cried and left bunches of flowers for her. By the middle of the first day, there were over a thousand bunches outside Kensington Palace. By the end of the week, it was like a sea of flowers there. With the flowers there were cards and letters: 'To our sweet Princess – Thank you for the love you showed us all.' 'Queen of Hearts' and 'Princess of Love' were words that came up again and again. 'We'll never forget you,' the letters said.

And during that week, the mystery about the car crash was growing. When Trevor Rees-Jones, the bodyguard, finally woke up in hospital, he couldn't remember the accident. We now know that the driver, Henri Paul, had too much to drink that evening – far too much. But the paparazzi were driving too fast and too near, and the photographers' lights were too bright. Did they make it happen, too? And was there a second car in the crash? Some people even thought that it was murder. This was probably just a wild story, but there was still a mystery about the crash.

By the middle of the first day, there were over a thousand bunches of flowers outside Kensington Palace. By the end of the week, it was like a sea of flowers there.

Diana's funeral was on Saturday, 6 September 1997, one week after she died. On Friday night, thousands of people went to London. They stayed out all night, waiting for the morning, when her body would travel from Kensington Palace to Westminster Abbey. Kensington Palace Gardens were beautiful. It was a warm night, and there were flowers by every tree. People of all ages sat quietly together in little groups, remembering Diana.

Her funeral, like her wedding, brought famous people together from all over the world. Some were heads of governments, and others were her friends. Many were famous names from the worlds of film and music. All the Royal Family was there. Princes Charles, William and Harry walked behind Diana's body as it went into the church. Her sons gave her white flowers with a card that just said, 'Mummy'. In Hyde Park, crowds of thousands watched

*Diana's funeral was on Saturday, 6 September 1997,
one week after she died.*

the funeral on a big screen. Many cried as they listened to the words, and heard some of Diana's favourite music.

Earlier that summer, Diana looked after her friend Elton John at Gianni Versace's funeral. Now he sang at her funeral. It was a song that he once wrote about the filmstar, Marilyn Monroe. Marilyn and Diana were both 36 when they died. Elton changed the words for Diana.

'Goodbye England's rose,' he sang. She would always 'grow in our hearts'.

Then her brother, Charles, spoke about Diana. He remembered how kind and beautiful she was.

'Today is our chance to say thank you . . . We want you to know that life without you is very, very difficult.'

He was very angry with the paparazzi who gave her such a hard time. And he promised to try and help her sons in their future life.

The funeral car took Diana's body to the Spencer family home at Althorp, in Northamptonshire. People threw flowers in front of the car as it went past. At first, her family planned to bring her to the local church at Althorp, but then they decided against this. Thousands of visitors could make life too difficult for the small village. So, finally, they took Diana to a small island in a lake in the gardens of Althorp Park. Here her body lies in private, but once every year, visitors can come to see the place where she rests.

Diana's life is over, but her story is not. The way that she lived and died will change many things. Her life showed a new road for the Royal Family to take. She showed them a way to be nearer to the British people and to help with real problems in the modern world. When she died, we all remembered that life can be very short. Every one of us has to do our best with the time that we have.

'It's important to show love,' said Diana.

We need to remember this too.

EXERCISES

Vocabulary Work

Look back at the 'Dictionary Words' in this book. Make sure that you know the meaning of each word.

1 Find the second half of each sentence on the left from the list on the right.

a His grandfather died on Sunday   i the beautiful princess married the prince.

b Her little girl was crying   ii who are ill, homeless, or have other problems.

c At the end of the fairy tale   iii so she gave her a big hug.

d Charities try to help people   iv and the funeral is tomorrow.

2 Find the Dictionary Words which go in these sentences.

a Elton John is a very ... singer. There is a ... of the song he sang at Princess Diana's funeral about her ...

b When Diana married Prince Charles, she became part of the ... Family.

c Diana's parents did not have a happy ... and finally they ...

d Diana often smiled in ... but was unhappy in .... She had plenty of friends, but often felt ....

e In 1995, Diana decided to make an ... on television.

f After the trouble with Charles and Camilla, people in Britain often ask, 'Will Charles really be our ... King?'

Comprehension

Chapters 1–2

1 How many brothers and sisters did Diana have, and what were their names?
2 What happened when Diana was six years old?
3 What lessons did she like doing at school?
4 What jobs did she do in London?
5 How did Diana meet Prince Charles?
6 Where did she and Charles get married?
7 What was her wedding dress like?

Chapters 3–4

8 When Diana first made public appearances, what did she have to learn to do?
9 When was her first son born, and what names did his parents give him?
10 What did Diana do in New Zealand to show that she was friendly?
11 Where did the family live in London, and what was their home like?
12 What kind of illness did Diana have?
13 Who was Charles meeting secretly?
14 What happened on holiday in Switzerland, and how did Diana change her life after that?

Chapters 5–6

15 Some secret telephone calls became public. What were they?
16 The Queen said 1992 was a terrible year. What were some of the things that made it difficult for her?
17 What kind of people did Diana help in her charity work?
18 When did Diana's marriage finally end?
19 Who was her new boyfriend, and what family did he come from?
20 Where did the accident happen that killed Diana?
21 Where did they take her body after the funeral?

Discussion

1 Why did Charles marry Diana, and did he love her when they got married? Was it possible for their marriage to be happy, or was it too difficult?

2 How did the newspaper reporters and photographers change Diana's life? Did she die because of them? Do we need to change things in future, so that they can't follow people everywhere?

3 Are the British Royal Family like other royal families that you know about? Do they need to change? How can they work best in the modern world?

Writing

1 Write a letter to say 'goodbye' to Diana (150 words). Say what was important about her life, and what she meant to you and other people.

2 You are someone who Diana helped in her charity work. Say who you are, and how she helped you (100 words).

Review

1 When Diana died, what did you read about her in the newspapers, or watch it on television? What kind of a picture did this give of her life? Is it a true picture? Or did the accident change the way that we think about her?

2 If you could ask Diana questions about her life, what would they be? What do you want to know or understand better about her life? Why?